Wind is air in motion.

I can fly!

The **atmosphere** is all of the air around Earth.

There we all are!

PUFF

All About Air

EMILY KATE MOON

DIAL BOOKS FOR YOUNG READERS

For my two boys,
the wind beneath my wings.

DIAL BOOKS FOR YOUNG READERS
An imprint of Penguin Random House LLC, New York

First published in the United States of America by Dial Books For Young Readers,
an imprint of Penguin Random House LLC, 2024

Dial Books for young Readers & colophon are trademarks of Penguin Random House LLC.
The Penguin colophon is a registered trademark of Penguin Books Limited.
Visit us online at PenguinRandomHouse.com.

Library of Congress Cataloging-in-Publication Data is available.

Manufactured in China • ISBN 9780593617960 • 10 9 8 7 6 5 4 3 2 1
TOPL
Design by Jason Henry • Text set in Avenir
The art in this book was painted in India ink on paper. Puff was drawn in Procreate,
where Emily Kate Moon finger-painted his swirly shape. She created the
layering and final touches in Photoshop.

With thanks to Darlene Kehn for her time and expertise.

This is air.

Hello!

I'm Puff!

Puff lives here, on planet Earth.

He has been here since the very beginning.

Earth and I go way back!

No other planet around has air like ours.

I'm clearly unique!!

It is wild and cold out in space,
but Puff knows how to keep us safe and warm.

Puff and all his friends gather around our planet.

Let's protect our planet!

Like tiny shields, they protect us from dangerous things, like space rocks and radiation.

We've got you covered!

And like puffy little blankets, they hold in heat and keep out cold.

All tucked in...

Puff and his friends have some very important jobs here on Earth.

☑ shield
☑ warmth
☑ wind
☑ breath

They are always on the go!

Let's goooo!

The sun heats up Earth and the air around it.

Puff and his friends swirl and whirl around
so they are not too hot,
too cold,
or too squished!

Too hot!

Too cold!

Too squished!

When Puff and his friends move,
they become wind.

Being wind is a breeze!

And being wind is important.

I can fly!

It's how Puff stays cool and comfortable, and how he carries things around the world, like water.

Have you met Drop? She's water.

Everyone knows me!

Hi Drop!

Hi Puff!

We are besties and we work together.

Puff and Drop make the weather, the skies, and the seas.

Teamwork!!

That's how we have water on land and life on Earth!

That's how we have breathable water and life within it.

Plants need air too.
Luckily, they use it the opposite way we do—

Carbon delivery!

Thank you!

they take in the carbon we breathe out,
and they push out the oxygen we breathe in.

It's a great deal!
And Puff makes all those tiny,
important trades for us.

Here's your oxygen!

Here's your carbon!

Earthlings of all shapes and sizes depend on Puff.

Since every living thing needs to breathe,
Puff makes sure
  he gets
    everywhere!

I love to travel!

He even ventures to deep-sea trenches!

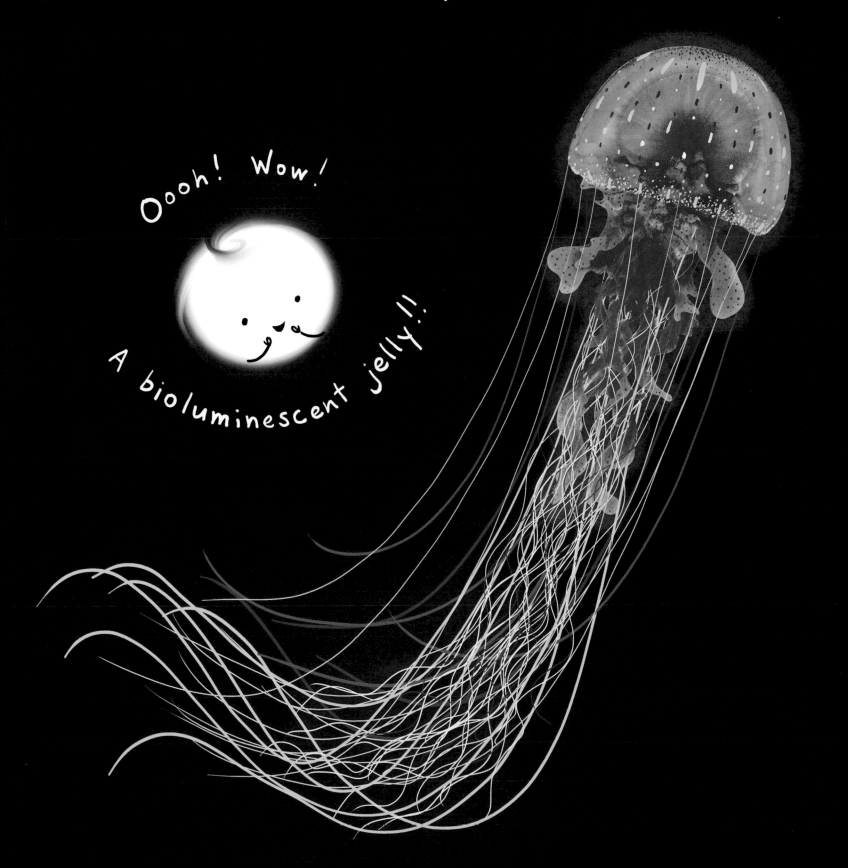

Oooh! Wow!
A bioluminescent jelly!!

And day and night,
Puff hosts life in the sky,

Come fly

where all sorts of airborne earthlings
float around with him.

with me!

Puff likes to keep things moving...

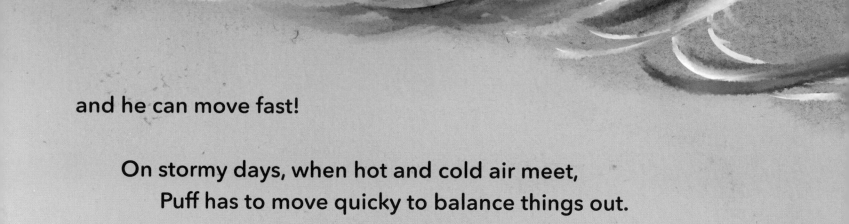

and he can move fast!

On stormy days, when hot and cold air meet,
   Puff has to move quicky to balance things out.

Sometimes, he gets going so fast,
   he spins out of control!

But most of the time, Puff cruises gently
from warm places to cooler places,

a warm desert wind...

and from cool places
to warmer places.

a cool ocean breeze...

And with him,
Puff carries
plant pollens and seeds,

from one place

Come on,
let's
go this way...

to another,

a little here...

a little there...

scattering them all around. . .

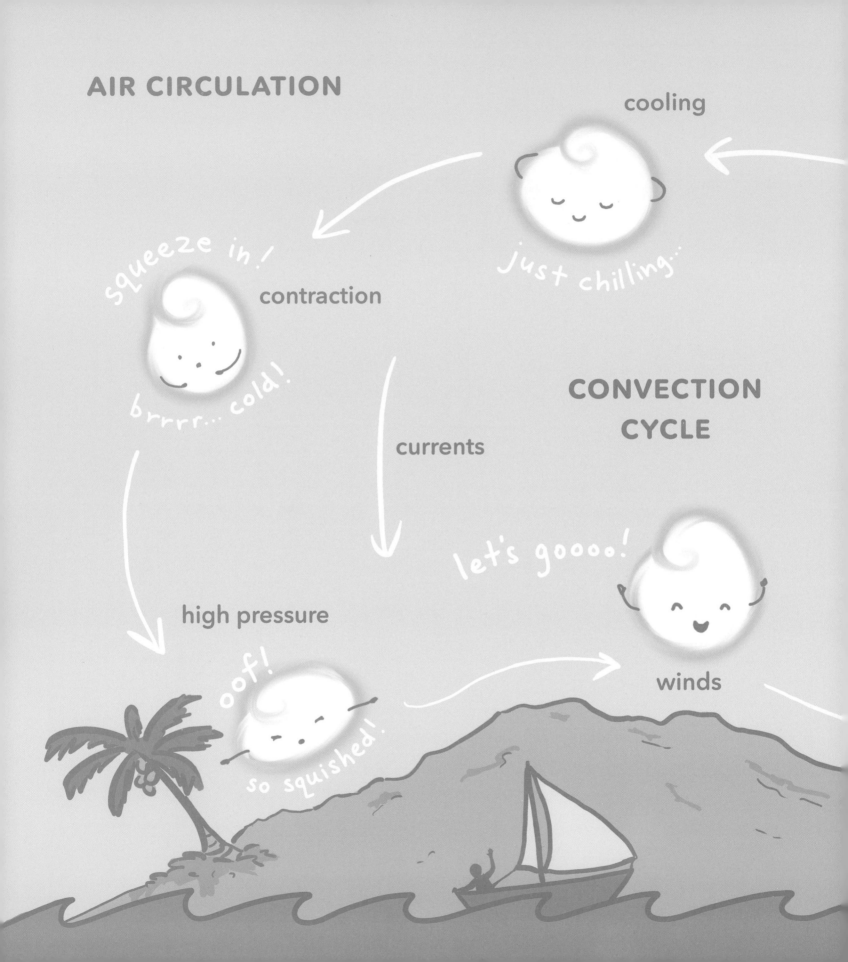